Chasing the Light

GRAND CANYON

"Don't only practice your art,
But force your way into its secrets,
for it and knowledge can raise
men to the divine."
~ Ludwig van Beethoven

Website: nationalparksusa.com
Email: parkpartnerorders@gmail.com
ISBN: 978-0-9842571-6-4
Printed in the Republic of South Korea
Poetic Text by Lynn Wilson
Publisher: Kevin Poulson
Canyon Notes by Jim Wilson
Introduction by Adam Schallau
Editor: Flora Massey
Book Design: Karen A. D'Amore, Fizzy Feather Designs

FOREWORD

by Adam Schallau

INTRODUCTION

In 1999 I made my first trip to the American Southwest to visit and explore our National Parks. This trip, planned as a 1-week excursion, had stops scheduled in the iconic locations including Grand Canyon National Park. My goal was to experience as much of the Southwest as possible in this short time.

After 2 days of driving, my wife and I arrived at the Grand Canyon. The sun was setting and we were running short on time. We quickly checked into our camp site at Mather Campground, and then found our way to the canyon's rim.

Seven years earlier, I had been living in Colorado working at a high-altitude field research station. I was surrounded by beautiful mountain peaks with fields of wildflowers and streams fed by melting snow. For a young man that had come from a big city in Texas, I was now living in a near-Utopian environment. Nothing could possibly be more beautiful.

I had felt this way for many years, and my longing for the mountains was strong. But now, as the sun was setting on the Grand Canyon and the shadows were growing long, the most subtle yet striking colors were being revealed, and in front of my very eyes a painting was coming to life.

Looking back on that evening, I don't remember much else. I don't recall being surrounded by the other park visitors standing on the rim. I don't recall making any adjustments to my camera's exposure settings. What does standout was an overwhelming sense of awe and peace.

This trip had an everlasting effect on us and would forever change our lives. Only 2 years later, Sally and I made the decision to quit our jobs and move to the Southwest to be closer to the landscape we love, and so that I could pursue photography as a profession. But with so many amazing locations to photograph, it still took another 7 years before we made it back to the Grand Canyon.

In May 2008, Sally and I made a trip to the Four Corners. At the same time, a late-season snow storm was pounding the region making travel quite difficult. We decided it was best to concentrate on one park to minimize the amount of driving we would be doing. We decided to go to the Grand Canyon.

We were greeted with an amazing site upon arriving at the Grand Canyon. Clouds were streaming off the many temples and buttes within the canyon, and as the light found its way between the clouds one part of the canyon would suddenly be illuminated while leaving the rest in shadow. We found ourselves, once again, standing on the rim of the Grand Canyon as a painting was being created before our very eyes.

We spent that week at the canyon hiking the rim, exploring every viewpoint, from Desert View in the east to the points along the Hermit Road in the west. I photographed every sunrise and every sunset, along the way studying how the light played across the land and how the weather interacted with the canyon. It was during this time that I was beginning to feel an unexplainable desire to be here, to experience the raw power and majesty of this landscape. It was the beginning of my romance with the Grand Canyon.

It was also during this visit in May 2008 that I learned about the National Park Service's Artist-in-Residence program. I wasn't yet a full-time artist, but the opportunity to live in the park, even for a short time, and concentrate on creating new work that could possibly generate understanding and dialogue about the need to preserve this national treasure, one of the seven natural wonders of the world, was very tempting. I promptly submitted my application upon returning home!

Several months went by, and in October 2008 I received a plain brown envelope from Grand Canyon National Park containing the letter I had been waiting for. I handed the letter to my wife to read this…"Congratulations on being selected as one of Grand Canyon National Park's 2009 Artist-in-Residence!"

In March 2009 I had my opportunity to be the park's Artist-in-Residence, and I've been photographing the canyon ever since. This has led to me moving to Flagstaff, Arizona to be closer to the canyon, and to become a full-time artist, and to lead guided photography workshops and expeditions at the Grand Canyon. All of this affords me the opportunity to spend countless days in the field every year in this place I love and to share with others what I love about it.

And now with each new year, new season, and new day, I find something fresh and stimulating to photograph here at the canyon. This primeval landscape carved by the mighty Colorado River and time has captured my heart.

GRAND CANYON NOTES

by Jim Wilson

THE COLORADO PLATEAU

In order to understand the Grand Canyon's origin one must first realize that this great feature is but a small, albeit important, piece of a much larger puzzle. The Canyon reflects the unleashed carrying and erosive power of the Colorado River and its tributaries. Located in the southwestern corner of a geological province scientists call the Colorado Plateau, this 130,000-square-mile geologic province teems with scenic treasures. Here water is both creator and sustainer of life. Although man-made highways cut through this region, allowing us easy access to Nature's handiwork, the network of watercourses that tentacle the province represent the true method of transportation. This network is dominated by the Colorado River and its tributaries.

On this high desert plateau water arrives infrequently. However, it is usually in quantities sufficient to spark flash flooding. This raw, unharnessed power is responsible, in large part, for carving the chasms seen throughout this region. In addition to water, the forces of cataclysmic uplift, grit-bearing winds, freeze-expansion-thaw and gravity have played contributing roles in sculpting the colorful ridges, mesas, buttes, pinnacles, bridges and arches of this land. Nearly two billion years of Earth's history can be observed in its canyons. Stories of ancient oceans, lakes, lagoons and deserts are revealed in multi-hued sedimentary layers. Ages of vulcanism are described in igneous rocks and unanswered questions can be found in metamorphic ones.

Elevation plays a major role here, ranging from over 12,000 feet in the La Sals and San Francisco Peaks to little more than 1,200 feet at the point where the Colorado River emerges from the Grand Canyon at Lake Mead. The biotic communities that exist on the Colorado Plateau are as diverse as these elevations would suggest.

VIEW FROM SOUTH RIM

When viewing this canyon, cut from western to eastern horizon, it seems obvious to the first-time visitor that erosion must have been the primary tool of creation for this deep chasm. This explanation works well to explain recent history, that of the past six million years. However, while marveling at its depth, one cannot help but notice the horizontal layering of various colored and textured rocks. A total of nearly 40 sedimentary and metamorphic rock formations have been identified, stacked one atop another revealing nearly two billion years of nature's handiwork. Scientists tell us the earth is 4.6 billion years old; here we can study more than one-third of this time period.

From South Rim the most obvious layers are those including, and above, the Tonto Plateau, that broad platform which stretches from the wall to the edge of the Inner Canyon. This upper 4,000 feet of the canyon was deposited during the Paleozoic era, from 250 to 550 million years ago.

These layers tell the story of the advance and retreat of no less than seven oceans, a Sahara-like desert and several lagoons. Below the Paleozoic strata are older, Pre-Cambrian rocks. These eight sedimentary strata, called the Grand Canyon Supergroup, include, among others, Shinumo Quartzite and Bass Limestone formations. Their ages are approximately one billion years. At some point after their creation, but before the overlying strata were laid down, the Grand Canyon Supergroup was broken into several tilted, north-to-south mountain ranges. Through the fault-blocking process portions of the Supergroup were uplifted while others dropped. Subsequent erosion removed all but the lowest of these blocks. This explains why we can observe only isolated pockets of this Supergroup throughout the length of Grand Canyon. The harder metamorphic and igneous rocks of the Inner Canyon were born of intense heat while the sedimentary history of the upper layers reflects a diverse series of quiet oceans, shallow seas, swamps, lagoons and wind-blown deserts.

After one's astonishment and sense of wonder settles in, one becomes aware that there is more to Grand Canyon National Park than a chasm. Life along the rim is rich and abundant. Ravens soar the thermals and squirrels scamper along the rim. The most basic forms of life one may observe are lichens and mosses both are well adapted to this semi-arid environment. Common shrubs include cliffrose, fernbush

and mountain mahogany. Forests of the South Rim are predominantly ponderosa pine, pinyon pine and Utah juniper. In addition, blooming throughout the summer season is a diverse variety of colorful wildflowers. The rim and surrounding forests are rich in wildlife, including mule deer, tassel-eared squirrels, black bear, wild turkey and various rodents, as well as many species of birds.

WHAT SHOULD THE FIRST-TIME VISITOR EXPECT?

Expect the unexpected!

*Hope for one small glimpse of insight,
one moment of breathless, speechless awe.
Hope for a vision of understanding, of wisdom.
Hope for "the sensation of the mystical.*

IT APPEARS TIMELESS AND UNCHANGING, *yet it is clear evidence of the changing nature of our planet. This landscape of sandstone, silt-stone, mudstone, limestone, shale, granite, schist and gneiss was left here by ancient oceans, swamps, lagoons, rivers and deserts.*

EDGE OF NOTHINGNESS
EXPANSIVE SPACE
IMMEASURABLY WIDE
UNFATHOMABLY DEEP
Utterly Quiet
Hauntingly peaceful

THIS PLACE IS A LIVING HISTORY BOOK.

The teacher of before.

Instructs me in the anatomy of

Today.

NOW.

HERE.

Time stands still.

Hours flash in moments.

Shadows grow to meet the rising moon.
Moonbeams dance across the land.
Stars chandelier the black of midnight.

BELOW THE RIM

Visitors descending below the South Rim encounter, one by one, the diverse layers of sediment laid down millions of years ago. First limestone, then sandstone, then shale. The question inevitably arises as to the differences between each layer. Science tells us that limestone results from the deposition of calcium carbonate, either from seawater or from dying prehistoric life forms such as trilobites, molluscs or brachiopods. These two sources, sometimes acting alone and sometimes together, combined with time and intense pressure, result in the formation of limestone. Sandstone is composed of grains of sand while shale is made up of silt and clay. Time, natural "cement" and pressure, mold each into unique layers of stone. Each has its own characteristics and reacts differently to erosion. Limestone and sandstone tend to form cliffs and ledges while shale, being weaker, tends to form slopes.

While descending alongside these multi-hued layers of sedimentary stone we are reminded that each layer was deposited many millions of years ago. "Millions of years ago" is a phrase that leaves most visitors glassy-eyed. For example, how can someone who is only able to trace his own ancestry but five generations fathom "millions of years ago". Let's take the Redwall Limestone formation. It is easy to understand that it is 400 to 650 feet thick, but as one saunters by trail, "through" the Redwall, keep in mind that it took 1 million to 1.6 million years to lay down this single formation. Also keep in mind that this layer was deposited approximately 330 million years ago.

How long in human terms is that? Today a human generation averages 25 years. One million years would see 40,000 human generations come and go. Standing in admiration of the great Redwall it is mind-boggling to think that 13.2 million human generations would have passed since its formation! As one continues to descend the trail alongside each sedimentary layer it becomes obvious that an incomprehensible amount of time has passed since they were deposited.

THE COLORADO RIVER

The first Europeans, members of Coronado's expedition, gazed into the Grand Canyon from near today's East Rim Drive. One of them estimated the river far below to be a mere six feet wide. Upon their return from a long, exhaustive and unsuccessful attempt at crossing the chasm several conquistadores told of a great wide river and rocks taller than the Tower of Seville. Modern "explorers", upon hiking the canyon or floating the river, experience this same awe-inspiring feeling. The river flowing deep in the canyon is the same one responsible for carving this chasm. As one peers into Grand Canyon from Yavapai Point it measures nearly ten miles from rim to rim and one mile deep.

How wide is ten miles? The world-famous Golden Gate Bridge is 1.5 miles long. If it were possible to connect the North Rim and the South Rims with a man-made span it would take seven Golden Gate Bridges constructed end to end. How deep is one mile? Horizontally, one mile of paved highway seems trivial, at 60 miles per hour a modern automobile will travel that one-mile in one minute. But one vertical mile surpasses five Empire State Buildings placed one atop another.

Interview any fatigued hiker as he emerges from a round trip hike to the Colorado River, he will surely have volumes to speak regarding that single vertical mile! Whether viewing or exploring the Grand Canyon, the question is asked "Where has the excavated earth gone?" The answer is it was, and continues to be, carried away by the Colorado River and its tributaries. The power of this river is illustrated by the fact that the excavation from the end of Marble Canyon to Grand Wash Cliffs was accomplished in just the last six million years. By geologic standards that is a relatively short period of time. It is difficult to comprehend how all the missing earth could have been moved by what appears to be a relatively insignificant body of water. However, a stream or river's ability to carry material away increases exponentially during flood stage.

It has been calculated that, prior to 1963, the average load moved by the Colorado was nearly 400,000 tons of earth per day. This means that if the load were placed in a series of five-ton dump trucks, it would require 80,000 trucks each 24-hour day to accomplish the same work carried out by the river. Still too great to imagine? Then consider that as you walk the Kaibab Suspension Bridge, on the way to Phantom Ranch, at the average rate of two miles per hour, nearly 139 of those dump trucks would have passed beneath your feet. With the completion of the Glen Canyon Dam in 1963, the wild and unpredictable river was harnessed and, consequently, its ability to move earth was greatly reduced. Today the average load is approximately 80,000 tons per day or only about one-fifth of its previous tonnage. The rock and sand extracted from Grand Canyon now lies downstream, behind Hoover Dam and on the floor of the Imperial Valley, creating the massive delta where the river empties into the Gulf of California.

The complete story of the creation of the Grand Canyon is still not fully understood, but suffice to say that the complex process continues, even as each visitor stands and gazes across to a distant rim.

NORTH RIM

The North Rim of Grand Canyon National Park is almost always described in comparison to South Rim: 'it is higher than...', 'it is less visited than...' or 'it is more isolated than...', etc. While those comparisons are correct, above all, North Rim is stunningly beautiful on its own merits. When visiting North Rim, keep in mind that the same forces created each rim, yet each rim possesses unique qualities. Exploring North Rim requires persistence. Some viewpoints along the Kaibab Plateau are accessible by paved road but all others, from Grand Wash Cliffs on the west to Grand Canyon Lodge on the east, require traveling many miles by foot or primitive road in order to reach the desired viewpoint.

North Rim is made up of four distinct plateaus, each a world unto itself. Rising from Grand Wash Cliffs is the Shivwits Plateau, a pinyon-juniper woodland interspersed with sage, yucca, cacti and some ponderosa pine. At approximately 5,000 feet in elevation, it is classified as a high desert. Separating Shivwits Plateau and its neighbor, Uinkaret Plateau, are the Hurricane Cliffs. Uinkaret is a wedge-shaped plateau which narrows as it approaches the canyon rim. Its environment is much like that of the Great Basin, containing vast stretches of sage, blackbrush and shadscale. Its most prominent features are the remnants of "recent" volcanic activity. Approximately one million years ago this area was an active volcanic zone, oozing molten lava from fissures opened by movement along fault zones.

To the east, Uinkaret is bounded by the Toroweap Fault and the Kanab Plateau, a flat, treeless plain most noted for the stunning water-cut chasm Kanab Creek has carved. The canyon slices through millenniums of sedimentary layers before joining the Colorado River. This plateau is home to large populations of deer, coyote and black-tailed jackrabbits.

At the eastern edge of the Kanab Plateau rises the uplifted Kaibab Plateau. This is the most visited area of North Rim. Lying between 7,000 and 9,000 feet above sea level it is the only area within the park where visitors can experience a lush subalpine spruce-fir forest. Kaibab Plateau is subjected to deep, cold winters, averaging 120 inches of annual snowfall, and cool summers. It is also home to a varied flora and fauna. Found here is the Kaibab squirrel, indigenous to the Kaibab Plateau. One can also observe mule deer, elk, bobcats and, if fortunate, mountain lions. Bird species include Williamson's sapsucker, western bluebird, black-tailed grosbeak, western meadowlark and, of course, the ever-present raven. High elevation and wet winters helped create, and still perpetuate, a series of montane meadows that support many species of grasses and colorful wildflowers. North Rim offers visitors unimaginable beauty as well as an ample supply of peace and solitude. It needs no comparison to any other area of the park or, for that matter, the Colorado Plateau.

The Grand Canyon is an incredible spectacle, a classic example of erosion unequalled anywhere on earth. It is the grand climax of the Colorado Plateau, the sum total of all the power nature has released into this geologic province. Grand Canyon is a park made up of many ecological worlds, including the subalpine forests of North Rim, the ponderosa pine forests of South Rim, the high desert-like Tonto Plateau and a Sonoran Desert environment at river level. In addition, there are untold micro-climes interspersed throughout, each possessing unique characteristics. One can be overwhelmed by a first visit to Grand Canyon and feel comfortable after several visits, but few, if any, have ever gained a complete mastery of all that this park encompasses. Its allure and complexities demand that one return again and again in order to satisfy the thirst for understanding.

Photo Captions
In order of appearance:

Front Cover
Lightning strikes the South Rim of Grand Canyon National Park near Hopi Point. Captured from Cape Royal on the North Rim of the park nearly 12 miles away. Zoroaster Temple is the prominent feature in the foreground.

Title Page:
Sunset from Lipan Point on the South Rim of the Grand Canyon.

Page 2:
Wotans Throne (left) and Vishnu Temple (right) being engulfed by clouds. Grand Canyon National Park.

Page 6:
The pastel light of a Summer sunrise illuminates the Grand Canyon.

Page 7:
Earth Shadow rises above the a winter scene at Grand Canyon National Park in Arizona.

Page 8:
Sunset from Powell Point at the Grand Canyon.

Page 9:
Looking along the Palisades of the Desert and down to the Colorado River. Grand Canyon National Park in Arizona.

Page 10:
Near the east end of Grand Canyon National Park, the Colorado River meanders around the Unkar Delta.

Page 12:
Looking out across a wintery Grand Canyon from the South Rim near Grandeur Point.

Page 13:
Rain falling into the Grand Canyon is backlit by the setting sun.

Page 15:
A sea of canyons. Grand Canyon National Park.

Page 16:
The Milky Way graces the night sky above the Watchtower at Desert View. Grand Canyon National Park in Arizona. To the right of the Watchtower is the Andromeda Galaxy, visible as a bright elliptical feature.

Sunlight shines through clouds illuminating Wotans Throne on the North Rim of Grand Canyon National Park in Arizona.

Page 17:
Looking through a pair of ponderosa pine trees to Mount Hayden from the North Rim of the Grand Canyon.

Page 18:
Dana Butte below Hopi Point. Grand Canyon National Park, Arizona.

Page 19:
Vishnu Temple amongst the clouds.

Early morning light strikes Yaki Point on the South Rim of the Grand Canyon.

Page 20:
Looking down Cedar Ridge to O'Neill Butte and the South Kaibab Trail and into the Grand Canyon from Yaki Point on the South Rim.

Page 21:
Sunrise near the 'Duck on a Rock' formation on the South Rim of Grand Canyon National Park.

Page 22:
Sunrise over the Grand Canyon from the South Rim. In the distance is the Colorado River.

Page 23:
The Colorado River as viewed from Mohave Point on the South Rim of Grand Canyon National Park.

Early morning light on the Grand Canyon from the South Rim of the park near El Tovar Lodge.

Page 24:
A late winter storm clears from Isis Temple in the Grand Canyon. Captured from Mather Point on the canyon's South Rim.

Page 26:
An agave rosette in Grand Canyon National Park.

Page 27:
The stalk of a Utah Agave. South Rim of Grand Canyon National Park.

Indian Paintbrush growing on the South Rim of Grand Canyon National Park.

A Utah Agave, Grand Canyon National Park.

Page 28 & 29:
A panoramic view of the Grand Canyon and the Colorado River from the South Rim.

Page 30:
The night sky above the Watchtower at Desert View. Grand Canyon National Park in Arizona.

Page 31:
The Milky Way above Grand Canyon National Park.

Page 32:
On May 20th, 2012, an annular solar eclipse occured and was visible from the Grand Canyon. The eclipse lasted a total of 4 minutes and 30 seconds, during which time the landscape was gently bathed in an eerie light with a subdued color palette...An annular solar eclipse occurs when the Moon passes between the Earth and the Sun, but the Moon's apparent diameter is smaller than that of the sun.

Page 33:
Sunlight breaks through the clouds and shines down onto the Colorado River. Viewed from Lipan Point on the East Rim Drive in Grand Canyon National Park.

Page 34:
Sunset from Mather Point on the South Rim of Grand Canyon National Park.

A cloudy day at the Grand Canyon.

Page 35:
The Palisades of the Desert along the East Rim of Grand Canyon National Park.

Page 36:
The Milky Way above the Grand Canyon.

Page 37:
The Watchtower at Desert View with a backdrop of a stormy sky. Grand Canyon National Park in Arizona.

Page 38:
Sunset on the Grand Canyon, viewed from Navajo Point on the East Rim drive near Desert View.

Page 39:
Lightning strikes the rim of the Painted Desert near the confluence of the Colorado River and the Little Colorado River.

Page 40 & 41:
A panoramic view of sunset at the Grand Canyon in Arizona.

Page 42:
Clouds begin to engulf Vishnu Temple in Grand Canyon National Park.

Page 43:
In what is known as a temperature inversion, clouds fill the Grand Canyon when cold air below the rim is trapped by warmer air above.

Page 45:
A hiker takes in the vista from atop some boulders on the South Rim of the Grand Canyon.

Page 46:
Sunrise near the 'Duck on a Rock' formation on the South Rim of Grand Canyon National Park.

Page 47:
The first rays of sunlight begin to illuminate the skies above the Painted Desert and the Watchtower at Desert View. Grand Canyon National Park in Arizona.

Page 48:
Clouds hover over the many rock formations found in the depths of the Grand Canyon.

Page 49:
Brahma and Zoroaster Temples emerge from the clouds. Grand Canyon National Park in Arizona.

Page 50:
Detail of the Watchtower at Desert View. Grand Canyon National Park.

Page 51:
Lightning strikes the Painted Desert of northern Arizona near the East Rim of Grand Canyon National Park.

Page 52:
Lightning from a summer thunderstorm strikes near the Colorado River. Grand Canyon National Park in Arizona.

Page 53:
A rainbow at the Desert View Watchtower, Grand Canyon National Park.

Page 54:
Early morning light on Mather Point on the South Rim of Grand Canyon National Park.

Page 55:
A winter storm at the Grand Canyon.

Page 56:
A bit of light breaks through the clouds to illuminate the rock walls of Grand Canyon National Park.

Early morning light strikes Angels Gate, Grand Canyon National Park in Arizona.

Page 57:
Sunrise from Yavapai Point, Grand Canyon National Park.

Page 58:
The Colorado River below the walls of the Grand Canyon.

Page 59:
The Colorado River emerges from Marble Canyon into the depths of the Grand Canyon.

Page 60:
Warm light fills the Grand Canyon.

Page 61:
Early morning on the rim of the Grand Canyon. Moisture fills the air as sunlight paints the temples and buttes of the canyon.

Page 62:
The interior of the Watchtower at Desert View. Grand Canyon National Park in Arizona.

Page 63:
Sunrise at the Desert View Watchtower in Grand Canyon National Park.

Page 64:
Sunrise from the South Rim of Grand Canyon National Park. In the distance, visible as a small ribbon of silver, is the Colorado River.

Sunset on Zuni Point. Grand Canyon National Park.

Page 65:
A rare weather phenomenon called a temperature inversion fills the Grand Canyon with clouds. This happens when cold air is trapped below the rim by hot air above. This particular event is very rare in that the entire canyon has been filled with fog, something which only happens once every 10 years.

Page 66 & 67:
The typically dry air of the Grand Canyon becomes soaked with the moisture of the monsoon season which runs from July through September. The monsoon brings cooling rains and dramatic skies to the Grand Canyon region.

Page 68:
Sunset from the South Rim of the Grand Canyon near Mather Point.

Page 69:
Full moon rising over the Grand Canyon as viewed from Hopi Point on the South Rim. Grand Canyon National Park, Arizona.

Page 70:
Looking down the Bright Angel Trail into the depths of the Grand Canyon.

Page 71:
Hikers on the Bright Angel Trail. Grand Canyon National Park, Arizona

Page 72:
Sunset on the Desert View Watchtower, South Rim, Grand Canyon National Park, Arizona.

Page 73:
In what is known as a temperature inversion, clouds fill the Grand Canyon when cold air below the rim is trapped by warmer air above.

Page 74:
A panoramic view of the Grand Canyon from the South Rim.

Page 75:
God beams fill the Grand Canyon with light with the Colorado River in shadow.

Page 76:
Lightning erupts from a thunderstorm, and the Milky Way graces the night sky above the Grand Canyon.

Page 77:
Rain falling into the Grand Canyon is backlit by the setting sun.

Page 78:
Lightning strikes the rim of the Painted Desert near the confluence of the Colorado River and the Little Colorado River.

Page 79:
A double rainbow forms on Brahma and Zoroaster Temples, in the Grand Canyon, after a summer thunderstorm.

Page 80:
The summer sky fills with puffy white clouds. Grand Canyon National Park in Arizona.

Morning light on the Grand Canyon and the Colorado River.

Page 81:
Sunrise over the Grand Canyon as viewed from Lipan Point. Grand Canyon National Park, Arizona.

Late spring brings rain to the Grand Canyon. From Mather Point on the South Rim of Grand Canyon National Park.

Page 82:
Afternoon sunlight shines through a light mist of rain filling the air in the Grand Canyon with a subtle glow.

Page 83:
A rain shower sweeps across the Grand Canyon. Desert View, Grand Canyon National Park, Arizona.

Page 84:
Sunrise over the Grand Canyon near the Desert View watchtower. Grand Ganyon National Park, northern Arizona.

Page 85:
Sunrise over Grand Canyon National Park as viewed from the Rim Trail near Mather Point.

Page 86:
Engine 4960, a steam train, delivering tourists to the South Rim of Grand Canyon National Park.

Page 87:
Mules waiting for their riders on. South Rim of Grand Canyon National Park.

Page 88 & 89:
The light of the setting sun paints hues of red and pink on the temples and thrones of the Grand Canyon.

Page 90:
A bull elk, also known as a wapiti, in the forest on the South Rim of Grand Canyon National Park in Arizona. His antlers are shedding their protective "velvet."

Page 91:
Grand Canyon viewed from Desert View.

Looking out across a wintery Grand Canyon from the South Rim near Grandeur Point.

Page 92:
A winter storm on Brahma and Zoroaster temples, Grand Canyon National Park in Arizona.

Sunrise from Yaki Point on the South Rim of Grand Canyon National Park.

Page 93:
In what is known as a temperature inversion, clouds fill the Grand Canyon when cold air below the rim is trapped by warmer air above.

Page 94:
Early evening light shines into the Grand Canyon National Park near Hopi Point on the Hermit Road on the park's South Rim.

Sunset on the Palisades of the Desert at Grand Canyon National Park.

Page 95:
The depths of the Grand Canyon display a rare green palette, the result of very rainy summer monsoon.

Page 96:
Brahma Temple and Zoroaster Temple in the clouds above the Grand Canyon.

Page 97:
Smoke from wildfires lends an unique beauty to the Grand Canyon.

Page 98:
Snow falling into the Grand Canyon.

Page 99:
A late winter snow blankets the forest on the South Rim of Grand Canyon National Park in Arizona.

Page 100:
Winter at the Desert View Watchtower in Grand Canyon National Park. A fresh blanket of snow is on the groud and the trees are covered in Rime ice.

Clouds rise out of the Grand Canyon after a winter storm leaves behind a fresh blanket of snow. In the distance is Cedar Mountain.

Page 101:
Monsoon skies over Brahma Temple and Zoroaster Temple.

Clouds form on Zoroaster Temple. Grand Canyon National Park.

Page 102:
The Night Sky, from Phantom Ranch at the bottom of Grand Canyon National Park.

The Milky Way above the ponderosa pine forest at Grand Canyon National Park.

Page 103:
Sunset on Angels Gate at the Grand Canyon in Arizona.

Page 104:
In what is known as a temperature inversion, clouds fill the Grand Canyon when cold air below the rim is trapped by warmer air above.

Page 105:
Sunset from Mather Point at the Grand Canyon.

Page 106:
A grand view of the Grand Canyon at sunset. From Lipan Point on the South Rim of Grand Canyon National Park.

Page 107:
Isis Temple, located in the Heart of the Grand Canyon. It is a prominent feature and is visible from Grand Canyon Village.

Page 108:
The Colorado River as viewed from Mohave Point on the South Rim of Grand Canyon National Park.

Page 109:
Monsoon skies over Brahma Temple and Zoroaster Temple.

Page 110:
The Colorado River gliding through the shadowy depths of the Grand Canyon.

Page 111:
Sunset from Yaki Point on the South Rim of Grand Canyon National Park.

A mist of rain illuminated by the setting sun in the Grand Canyon.

Page 112:
The Grand Canyon from Pipe Creek Vista on the South Rim.

Page 113:
Sunrise on Battleship Rock. From Yavapai Point, Grand Canyon National Park.

Page 114:
A moody sunrise from the South Rim of Grand Canyon National Park.

Page 115:
Sunset on the Grand Canyon as viewed from Hopi Point on the South Rim.

Page 116:
Early morning at the Grand Canyon.

Page 117:
Sun beams in the Grand Canyon.

Page 118:
Looking towards Powell Point and Wotans Throne from Hopi Point on the South Rim of the Grand Canyon.

A fresh snowfall blankets the South Rim of Grand Canyon National Park near Mather Point.

Page 119:
Winter on the South Rim of Grand Canyon National Park in Arizona.

Early morning light on the Grand Canyon from the South Rim of the park near El Tovar Lodge.

Page 120:
Lightning erupts from a summer thunderstorm over the Grand Canyon and the Colorado River.

Page 121:
Sunset from Hopi Point on the South Rim.

Sunset over the Grand Canyon and the Colorado River from Mohave Point on the South Rim.

Page 122:
Sunset at the Grand Canyon from Powell Point.

Page 123:
Sunset on the Grand Canyon as viewed from Yavapai Point on the South Rim.

Page 124:
Brahma and Zoroaster Temples in the clouds above the Grand Canyon.

Page 125:
A winter scene of the Grand Canyon. From the South Rim near Grandeur Point.

Page 126:
The view from Plateau Point in Grand Canyon National Park.

Page 127:
Sagebrush, Grand Canyon National Park.

Page 128:
The Colorado River as viewed from the bottom of the Grand Canyon near Phantom Ranch. In the distance is the "Black" bridge crossing the river from the South Kaibab Trail.

Page 129:
Native American pictographs in Grand Canyon National Park.

Page 130:
Bright Angel Creek just past Phantom Ranch. In the distance is the 'Black Bridge' one of two foot bridges which cross the Colorado River. Grand Canyon National Park.

Sunrise from the South Rim of Grand Canyon National Park. In the distance, visible as a small ribbon of silver, is the Colorado River.

Page 131:
Early morning light on Mather Point on the South Rim of Grand Canyon National Park.

Page 132:
Confluence of Bright Angel Creek and the Colorado River.

Page 133:
A small cabin near Phantom Ranch at the bottom of the Grand Canyon. Grand Canyon National Park, Arizona.

The sun begins to set on the Inner Gorge of Grand Canyon National Park near Phantom Ranch. In the distance is the Silver Bridge, one of two foot bridges over the Colorado River.

Page 134:
Desert flora at the bottom of the Grand Canyon.

Looking through the mist of Ribbon Falls out to the depths of the Grand Canyon.

Page 135:
The view from Plateau Point in Grand Canyon National Park.

Page 136:
Sunset at Toroweap in the Tuweep Ranger District of Grand Canyon National Park.

Page 138:
Cardenas Butte overlooking the Colorado River. Grand Canyon National Park in Arizona.

Page 140:
Hikers on the Bright Angel Trail. Grand Canyon National Park, Arizona

Page 141:
The Colorado River upstream in Glen Canyon Recreational Area.

Page 142:
Looking down from the Navajo Bridge onto the Colorado River in Marble Canyon near Lees Ferry, the starting point for many rafting trips into the Grand Canyon.

Page 144:
Afternoon light in the Grand Canyon and Colorado River.

Page 145:
The warmth of the summer sun illuminates the depths of the Grand Canyon reaching all the way down to the Colorado River.

Page 146:
A photographer stands on the edge of Grand Canyon at Toroweap.

Sunrise on the Grand Canyon and the Colorado River.

Page 147:
The Colorado River in the depths of the Grand Canyon.

Page 148:
Rain falling near the Colorado River in the Grand Canyon.

Page 149:
The Colorado River in the Grand Canyon.

Hance Rapids as seen from Lipan Point in Grand Canyon National Park.

Page 150:
The Colorado River upstream in Glen Canyon Recreational Area in Page, Arizona.

Page 151:
The Colorado River at the bottom of the Grand Canyon.

Page 152:
Sunlight shines through clouds illuminating the depths of the Grand Canyon. From Cape Royal on the North Rim.

Page 154:
Beams of sunlight known as Anti-Crespecular Rays pass over the North Rim of the Grand Canyon towards the Painted Desert.

Page 155:
A gentle rain falls on the North Rim during the pre-dawn light.

Page 156:
Summer rains fall into the Grand Canyon.

Page 158:
An aerial view of the snow covered burn area on the North Rim of Grand Canyon National Park. Aspens, which can be seen here as the bright green area, are often some of the first trees to grow after a forest fire.

The recovery of a wildfire fire burn area on the North Rim of Grand Canyon National Park.

Page 159:
Sunrise on Mount Hayden, as viewed from Point Imperial on the North Rim of Grand Canyon National Park.

Page 160:
The pink light of sunset brings an ethereal glow to the cliffs of Toroweap, 3,000 feet above the Colorado River. Grand Canyon National Park, Arizona.

Page 161:
The Colorado River as viewed from Toroweap. Grand Canyon National Park.

Page 162:
A winter scene deep within the forest on the South Rim of Grand Canyon National Park in Arizona.

Page 163:
A winter scene, Grand Canyon National Park.

Page 164:
Ribbon Falls, Grand Canyon National Park, Arizona.

Beautiful Ribbon Falls on the North Rim of Grand Canyon National Park.

Page 165:
Detail of Ribbon Falls, North Rim, Grand Canyon National Park.

Page 166:
Grand Canyon sunset from Cape Royal.

Page 167:
Lightning strikes the South Rim of Grand Canyon National Park near Hopi Point. Captured from Cape Royal on the North Rim of the park nearly 12 miles away. Zoroaster Temple is the prominent feature in the foreground.

Page 168:
A summer monsoon thunderstorm advances across Bright Angel Canyon in Grand Canyon National Park.

Page 169:
Navajo Mountain seen from Point Imperial, over 80 miles away, on the North Rim of Grand Canyon National Park.

Page 170:
Angels Window on the North Rim of Grand Canyon National Park.

A view to Vishnu Temple from an unnamed point on the North Rim near Cape Final.

Page 171:
Tritle Peak as seen from Roosevelt Point on the North Rim of Grand Canyon National Park in Arizona.

Page 172:
The trail out to Bright Angel Point on the North Rim of Grand Canyon National Park.

Page 173:
A Grand Canyon sunset from Bright Angel Point on the North Rim.

3,000 feet above the Colorado River at Toroweap. In the Tuweep District of Grand Canyon National Park.

Page 174:
A rainbow ends at the Grand Canyon. From Point Imperial on the North Rim, the highest point in Grand Canyon National Park at 8,803 feet above sea-level. The prominent peak in the foreground is Mount Hayden.

The view east from Cape Royal on the North Rim of Grand Canyon National Park.

Sunset over Mount Hayden from Point Imperial on the North Rim of Grand Canyon National Park.

Page 175:
Sunrise on Mt. Hayden. North Rim of Grand Canyon National Park.

Page 176:
Wotans Throne viewed from Cape Royal on the North Rim of Grand Canyon National Park.

Page 177:
Mount Hayden on the North Rim of Grand Canyon National Park.

Page 178:
Looking through a pair of ponderosa pine trees to Mount Hayden from the North Rim of the Grand Canyon.

Trees hang onto the steep slopes of the North Rim of the Grand Canyon.

Page 179:
Mount Hayden at sunrise. As viewed from Point Imperial on the North Rim of Grand Canyon National Park.

Page 180:
Sunset over Mount Hayden from Point Imperial on the North Rim of Grand Canyon National Park.

Page 181:
Sunset over Grand Canyon National Park and the Colorado River from Toroweap.

Page 189:
A brilliant sunset from the North Rim of Grand Canyon National Park.

Page 190:
The clouds begin to lift moments before sunset revealing Wotans Throne. From Cape Royal on the North Rim of Grand Canyon National Park.

 ADAM SCHALLAU is an award-winning fine art photographer best known for his landscapes of the American West. He expresses his passion for the American landscape through his photography, revealing intimate details and awe inspiring vistas while working in the margins of light as the landscape comes to life in an explosion of color.

His work has been highly-recognized by Nature's Best Photography—the Windland Smith Rice Awards, and he has received top-honors in the New Mexico Magazine and Arizona Highways photo contests. He is a recipient of the Luminous Landscape Endowment, and he was the Winter 2009 Artist-in-Residence at Grand Canyon National Park.

Adam's photographs have appeared on the covers of magazines, calendars, music CDs, and in numerous publications, including Arizona Highways, Sunset Magazine, Backpacker, New Mexico Magazine, and Men's Journal. His images have been used by many companies and organizations, including Apple, B&H Photo, CNN, New Mexico Land Conservancy, New Mexico Wilderness Alliance,

Our Texas Wild, National Audubon Society, Grand Canyon Association, and the National Park Service. His fine art prints are in personal and corporate collections across the world, and they have been exhibited in numerous galleries, museums, and National Parks.

His work has been used in support of environmental and conservation awareness issues including the protection of the Valle Vidal in New Mexico. He also volunteers his time, knowledge, and enthusiasm to the Parks in Focus program who's mission is to provide opportunities for middle school youth from underserved communities to explore and learn about nature through photography, outdoor education, and creative expression.

Adam owns and operates a photography workshop business guiding photo workshops and tours at Grand Canyon National Park for photographers of all levels. He lives in a cabin in the ponderosa pine forest of northern Arizona near the mountain town of Flagstaff, with his wife Sally, and their dog Ouray.